# BILL & TED's MOST EXCELLENT
## MOVIE BOOK

Published in 2020 by Welbeck
An Imprint of Welbeck Non-Fiction Limited, part of Welbeck Publishing Group
20 Mortimer Street, London W1T 3JW

Text and Design © 2020 Welbeck Non-Fiction Limited

A CIP catalogue record for this book is available from the British Library

978 1 78739 441 4

Printed in Italy

10 9 8 7 6 5 4 3 2 1

# BILL & TED's MOST EXCELLENT MOVIE BOOK

**LAURA SHAPIRO**

FOREWORD BY
CHRIS MATHESON AND ED SOLOMON

WELBECK

"STRANGE THINGS
ARE AFOOT AT
THE CIRCLE K."

– TED

# CONTENTS

# FOREWORD
## CHRIS MATHESON AND ED SOLOMON

Writing *Bill & Ted's Excellent Adventure* was a different experience of creation than any we've had. It was remarkable how, from the moment they appeared, it was like something better than us had come to life within us and we just were following them forward. Even though our first impulse was to make fun of them (they emerged from the improv suggestion "let's do guys who know nothing about history studying history"), the instant they landed on our shoulders we knew there was nothing to make fun of. They were sweet, big-hearted, very tolerant, very intuitive. They had crazy ideas that sort of bizarrely worked out. They found pretty much everything in the world excellent.

We've always felt we could put Bill and Ted anywhere and we'd know what they'd say. And if we didn't – they'd tell us. If they were stuck in a blank, windowless room for eternity, they'd somehow keep each other entertained. That's why the phrase "Be excellent to each other" just popped out. Because it wasn't us – it was Bill and Ted. It seemed so silly – ridiculous, even – at the time. But now, looking back, of course that's what they would say.

Alex and Keanu not only understood intuitively, but they embodied the characters with so much depth and affection that in the same way that we passed Bill and Ted onto them, they, in turn, passed them on to the world. Which is the most amazing thing of all; that this thing that started as a lark in a tiny underground space one night nearly four decades ago has found enough of a place in our culture that we all had a chance to inhabit these characters one last time. For that, we're just thankful that on that night that Bill and Ted arrived and started talking to us, we had enough sense to at least stop for a moment and listen to them.

Chris Matheson & Ed Solomon, May 2020

"ALEX AND KEANU NOT ONLY UNDERSTOOD INTUITIVELY, BUT THEY EMBODIED THE CHARACTERS WITH SO MUCH DEPTH AND AFFECTION THAT IN THE SAME WAY THAT WE PASSED BILL AND TED ONTO THEM, THEY, IN TURN, PASSED THEM ON TO THE WORLD."

CHRIS & ED

# INTRODUCTION
## THE EXCELLENT ADVENTURE BEGINS

BILL & TED WERE BORN IN 1983 WHEN RECENT COLLEGE GRADS AND BEST FRIENDS CHRIS MATHESON AND ED SOLOMON STARTED AN IMPROV GROUP WITH A FEW OF THEIR FRIENDS. THEY RENTED A TINY BASEMENT THEATER ON SUNSET BOULEVARD IN HOLLYWOOD AND PROCEEDED TO TRY TO MAKE EACH OTHER LAUGH. THEY HAD NO AUDIENCE BUT EACH OTHER.

The improv prompt was: two teenage boys who don't know anything about history (or anything else). Chris was Ted, Ed was Bill, or maybe it was the other way around – no one remembers for sure. "I can't remember that either one of us in in any specific conscious way was either." Chris Matheson says. "I think we were both. They're not the same person, but they're close enough that they're pretty similar and they think the same way. They're just always thinking more or less the same thing," And they were off, riffing on history's greatest hits, cracking each other up. The next year as they ventured out into the world post college, Chris to graduate school for theater directing, Ed to his first industry job as a staff writer for the TV show *Laverne & Shirley*, they kept Bill & Ted alive by writing each other letters in character.

**Above:** Chris Matheson and Ed Solomon performing Bill & Ted at Dykstra Hall, UCLA, as part of the UCLA Comedy Workshop, c. 1983.

**Opposite:** Bill and Ted atop their time traveling phone booth. Promotional shot for *Excellent Adventure*.

In summer of 1984 they hunkered down at Norms, an all night diner in Los Angeles, and started writing the script that became *Bill & Ted's Excellent Adventure*. Originally the phone booth was a van, driven by Rufus, a 27-year-old homeless high school sophomore who lived in his van, accompanied by his dog, Dog-Rufus.

Ed Solomon was at a pivotal point in his young life: "I got a job on a TV show right out of college and became very disillusioned about what being a professional writer meant; I wondered if I had the fortitude to stay in it. Chris and I decided to write a screenplay together and we thought, what if we expanded these characters that we'd been playing around with? Initially it was Bill and Ted juxtaposed with the greatest people who ever lived. That was the original core concept of the movie. We had so much fun writing it that it re-inspired me creatively to follow what made me laugh rather than where I could find a job.

'We wrote Bill and Ted with a divining rod toward only what made us laugh, and that changed my life. My agents didn't get it. They fired me. And thank God they did, because the new agent got it, and it really did ignite our careers."

The film found a home at Interscope in December of '84. Robert Cort, the president of the company, hired young executive Scott Kroopf, who championed the project. "In 1984 when I got hired to work at Interscope, they asked me 'What's the best script you've read lately?', I immediately said, Bill & Ted," recalls Kroopf. It was initially developed at Warner Bros., where the van became a phone booth when executives thought the van was too similar to the Delorean in *Back to the Future*. (None of the Americans involved had yet heard of *Doctor Who*.)

## CAST

```
Ted "Theodore" Logan.......................KEANU REEVES
Bill S. Preston............................ALEX WINTER
Rufus......................................GEORGE CARLIN
Napoleon...................................TERRY CAMILLERI
Billy the Kid..............................DAN SHOR
Socrates...................................TONY STEEDMAN
Freud......................................ROD LOOMIS
Genghis Khan...............................AL LEONG
Joan of Arc................................JANE WIEDLIN
Abraham Lincoln............................ROBERT V. BARRON
Beethoven..................................CLIFFORD DAVID
Captain Logan..............................HAL LANDON, JR.
Mr. Ryan...................................BERNIE CASEY
Missy/Mom..................................AMY STOCK-POYNTON
Mr. Preston................................J. PATRICK McNAMARA
Deacon.....................................FRAZIER BAIN
Princess Joanna............................DIANE FRANKLIN
Princess Elizabeth.........................KIMBERLEY LaBELLE
Ox.........................................WILL ROBBINS
Randolf....................................STEVE SHEPHERD
Buffy......................................ANNE MACHETTE
Jody.......................................TRACI DAWN DAVIS
Bartender..................................DUNCAN McLEOD
Tatooed Cowboy.............................JOHN CLURE
Bearded Cowboy.............................JIM CODY WILLIAMS
Old West Ugly Dude.........................DUSTY O'DEE
Kerry......................................HEATHER PITTMAN
Daphne.....................................RUTH PITTMAN
Bowling Alley Manager......................DICK ALEXANDER
John the Serf..............................JAMES BOWBITCH
Evil Duke..................................JOHN KARLSEN
Mother at Waterslides......................JEANNE HERMINE HEREK
Waterslide Attendant.......................JONATHAN BOND
Music Store Salesman.......................JEFF S. GOODRICH
Girl at Mall...............................LISA RUBIN
Student Speaker............................MARJEAN HOLDEN
Aerobic Saleswoman.........................CLAUDIA TEMPLETON
Aerobic Instructor.........................CAROL GOSSLER
Mall Photographer..........................J. DONOVAN NELSON
Store Clerk................................MARCIA DARROCH
Police Psychiatrist........................STEVE ROTBLATT
Stupid Waiter..............................ED SOLOMON
Ugly Waiter................................CHRIS MATHESON
Neanderthal #1.............................MARK OGDEN
Neanderthal #2.............................TOM DUGAN
Security Guard.............................RON R. ALTHOFF
The Three Most Important
   People In the World.....................MARTHA DAVIS
                                           FEE WAYBILL
                                           CLARENCE CLEMONS
```

DE LAURENTIIS ENTERTAINMENT GROUP

PRESENTS

IN ASSOCIATION WITH DE LAURENTIIS FILM PARTNERS L.P.


AN
INTERSCOPE
COMMUNICATIONS
PRODUCTION


IN ASSOCIATION WITH
SOISSON/MURPHEY
PRODUCTIONS


"BILL & TED'S EXCELLENT ADVENTURE"


KEANU REEVES
ALEX WINTER


Co-starring
ROBERT V. BARRON     AL LEONG
TERRY CAMILLERI     ROD LOOMIS
CLIFFORD DAVID     DAN SHOR


TONY STEEDMAN
JANE WIEDLIN


BERNIE CASEY


AND
GEORGE CARLIN
AS RUFUS

Original Score by DAVID NEWMAN
Edited by LARRY BOCK and PATRICK RAND
Production Designer ROY FORGE SMITH
Director of Photography TIMOTHY SUHRSTEDT
Executive Producers TED FIELD and ROBERT W. CORT
Written by CHRIS MATHESON & ED SOLOMON
Produced by SCOTT KROOPF, MICHAEL S. MURPHEY, JOEL SOISSON
Directed by STEPHEN HEREK


MPAA RATING:   PG             RUNNING TIME: 91 minutes

| NO. | DESCRIPTION | MUSIC & EFFECTS | NO. | DIALOGUE & SPOTTING LIST | START | FINISH | TOTAL |
|---|---|---|---|---|---|---|---|
| 13. | (CONTINUED...) | RUMBLING SOUND CONT. | 31. | RUFUS: (CONT.) ...the two great ones...ran into a few problems. | 246.06 | 251.10 | 5.4 |
| | | | 32. | So now, I have to travel back in time to help them out. | 252.03 | 256.04 | 4.1 |
| | THE SQUARE IMAGE ON THE R. GROWS TO COVER THE WHOLE FRAME & BRIGHT WHITE LIGHT HITS THE IMAGE WHICH DISAPPEARS BEHIND IT AS DOES RUFUS. | LOUD SWISH. | | | | | |
| | FADE IN FROM WHITE - M.S. OF BILL & TED ON VIDEO PLAYING THEIR GUITARS. | LOW GUITAR MUSIC IN. VIDEO STATIC IN. | 33. IT | RUFUS: (V.O.) If I should fail to keep these two on the correct path, | 257.14 | 261.12 | 3.14 |
| 14. | 262+1 L.S. OF BILL & TED PRACTICING THEIR GUITARS W/THEIR IMAGE ON VIDEO IN BCKGRD. INT. GARAGE - DAY. | | 34. IT | (V.O.) ...the basis of our society will be in danger. | 262.07 | 265.07* | 3.0 |
| 15. | 265+8 M.S. OF VIDEO CAMERA BEING RAISED UP BY TED WHO PUTS IT TO HIS EYE AS HE MOVES TOWARDS THE L. BCKGRD. | | 35. IT | (V.O.) Don't worry. It'll all make sense. I'm a professional. | 265.14 | 270.0* | 4.2 |
| 16. | 270+2 M.C.U. OF BILL PLAYING HIS GUITAR. CAMERA JUMPS DOWN TO HIS GUITAR & BACK UP TO HIM MOVING IN & OUT OF C.U. TED'S VIDEO CAMERA'S P.O.V. | GUITAR MUSIC UP. | 36. | BILL: I'm Bill S. Preston, Esquire. | 271.10 | 275.12 | 4.2 |
| 17. | 276+0 M.S. OF TED HOLDING VIDEO CAMERA UP TO HIS EYE. HE LOOKS DOWN, THEN UP. | | 37. | TED: And I'm Ted the... Oh wait...Bill? | *276.0 | 280.14* | 4.14 |

# Bill & Ted's EXCELLENT adventure

"IT WAS MY SECOND MOVIE. I WASN'T THAT MUCH OLDER THAN KEANU AND ALEX WHEN I MADE IT," DIRECTOR STEPHEN HEREK RECALLS. "THEY WANTED TO MAKE THE MOVIE FOR A VERY SMALL AMOUNT OF MONEY, BUT WE COULDN'T MAKE IT FOR THAT PRICE... ROBERT CORT DID SOMETHING REALLY QUITE MAGICIAN-LIKE. HE GOT WARNER'S TO GIVE HIM A TWO-DAY TURN AROUND OVER A WEEKEND, SO HE COULD SHOP THE FILM AROUND."

performing in a prom
which has been lost

During that weekend, Cort got Dino De Laurentiis' company interested in it. Dino, being non-union, could make it for less money than Warner's. So it all changed hands pretty much overnight."

DEG's European base gave the modestly budgeted film increased production values, including shooting in Europe, particularly Rome, the home of DEG. "Rafaella De Laurentiis hooked us up in Rome. She called in favors with everyone they knew and significantly upped the production value, which made making the movie even more thrilling," Kroopf remembers. Young stars Keanu Reeves and Alex Winter were cast, along with legendary comedian George Carlin as Rufus, now a cool messenger from the future come to help Bill & Ted fulfill their destiny – to write the song that saves the world – but only if they can pass their history test!

Alex Winter recalls the shoot as a youthful, joyful experience, "I'd been acting since I was a little kid, and I was fresh out of film school. I'd just done *Lost Boys* and had fallen into the audition process for this thing without really knowing much about it or the people behind it. Everybody was so young. Chris and Ed were really young; they're only a few years older than I am. I was only 20, maybe 21. Stephen Herek (the director) I think, was 27, maybe five, six years older than me. Really a bunch of kids, to be honest. Dino De Laurentiis had put faith in it, but not a ton of money, and I don't think we really knew what the hell it was. We all sort of felt like we were getting away with something."

But, as Herek recalled, that was the "honeymoon phase" of the project. "We came back and all was good, we're cutting it, moving along. About six

**Above:** Bill & Ted's most excellent gesture. Promo shot.

**Opposite, top:** Bill & Ted's most excellent gesture, with San Dimas High cheerleaders and football players. Promo shot.

**Opposite, below:** Production shot of Bill & Ted and the Historical Figures in the phone booth.

weeks into editing – the movie was still about two hours, twenty minutes long – our special effects company went bankrupt. Special effects at the time were not computer generated, but we did have a company helping with the 'circuits of time'; it was sort of experimental because nobody was really doing it that way. We couldn't finish any of it.. This is where everything started to go to shit." De Laurentiis rushed them into an industry preview, with no effects and a partially edited film that was too long. Nobody liked it.

"We were working at CFI – Dino had a lot of cutting rooms there. All of a sudden we started seeing equipment being moved out of other rooms. They were shutting him down. We started locking our doors, because we heard about what was going on, but we didn't know exactly what was happening. We eventually got the word: Dino was bankrupt," Herek recalls.

There was an output deal to HBO for a very small amount of money, and for a time that seemed to be Bill & Ted's fate. Scott Kroopf had been working closely with DEG's head of legal, Rick Finklestein, to save the film for a theatrical release. Rick moved on to Nelson Entertainment after the bankruptcy and picked the film up. "Barry Spikings, head of Nelson Entertainment, thought the film was a hoot, and said, 'What the hell, I'll take a chance on it,'" recalls Kroopf. Nelson Entertainment had a relationship with Orion Pictures, who distributed the film.

"We started editing again and I got it down to somewhere in the neighborhood of 95 minutes, and got some temp effects in so the people could at least see what the hell was going on. We did a preview, and it went through the roof. People were going crazy for this movie, applauding, laughing," Herek recalls.

The film was finally released 1989. It was a moderate hit, and slowly in those pre-internet days, began to develop a cult following.

**Right (top and below):** Bill & Ted rock out in the garage.

**Right (center):** Bill S. Preston's homemade Wyld Stallyns sweatshirt.

**Opposite (top):** Bill & Ted's history teacher, Mr. Ryan, tells them they will fail history if they don't get an A on their report.

**Opposite (left):** Bill & Ted load up on books.

**Opposite (right):** Mr. Ryan teaches history at San Dimas High.

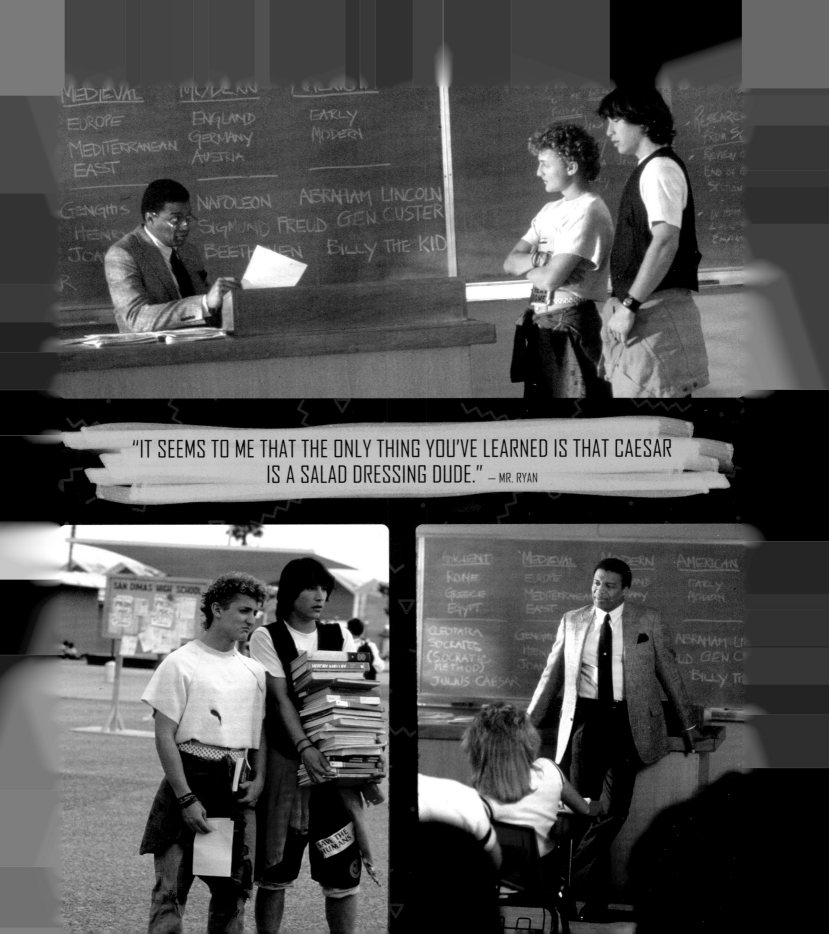

"IT SEEMS TO ME THAT THE ONLY THING YOU'VE LEARNED IS THAT CAESAR IS A SALAD DRESSING DUDE." — MR. RYAN

**Above:** Bill & Ted see the time traveling phone booth for the first time at the Circle K.

**Below:** Rufus, with both phone booths, observes the arrival of slightly older Bill & Ted,

**Opposite:** Bill & Ted (and the Historical Figures) hurtle through time in the phone booth.

Stills from the deleted—and lost—prom scene that was originally featured at the end of *Excellent Adventure*.

# BILL S. PRESTON, ESQUIRE/ALEX WINTER

"TED, WHILE I AGREE THAT, IN TIME, OUR BAND WILL BE MOST TRIUMPHANT. THE TRUTH IS, WYLD STALLYNS WILL NEVER BE A SUPER BAND UNTIL WE HAVE EDDIE VAN HALEN ON GUITAR." — BILL

# TED "THEODORE" LOGAN/KEANU REEVES

"NOW TED, WHO WAS JOAN OF ARC?" — MR. RYAN
"NOAH'S WIFE?" — TED

"DEACON, DO YOU REALIZE YOU HAVE JUST STRANDED ONE OF EUROPE'S GREATEST LEADERS IN SAN DIMAS?" — TED
"HE WAS A DICK!" — DEACON

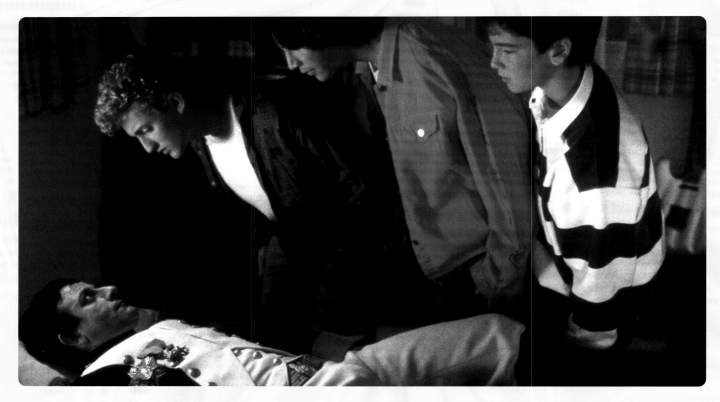

**Previous pages (below left):** Writers Chris Matheson and Ed Solomon – in cameos as "Ugly Waiter" and "Stupid Waiter" – taunt Napoleon.

**Top:** Bill & Ted and Deacon wake Napoleon from his nap.

**Left:** Napoleon at the bowling alley.

**Above:** Napoleon at the water park: "If we were one of the greatest generals in history and we were stranded in San Dimas for one day, where would we go?" "Waterloo!"

**Opposite (below):** Napoleon lays out his battle plan for Bill & Ted as part of their high school presentation.

# BEETHOVEN/CLIFFORD DAVID

"MRS PRESTON, WE'D LIKE YOU TO MEET SOME OF OUR FRIENDS" — TED
"THIS IS, UH, DAVE BEETH OVEN." — BILL

**Above:** Beethoven instructs Ted in music theory in a cut scene.

**Left:** Beethoven helps clean Bill's house.

**Opposite:** Beethoven ("Are you a musician?") impresses in the music store at the mall.

"BEETHOVEN'S FAVORITE WORKS INCLUDES MOZART'S *REQUIEM*, HANDEL'S *MESSIAH*, AND BON JOVI'S *SLIPPERY WHEN WET*."

– BILL

# SOCRATES/TONY STEEDMAN

"ALL WE ARE IS DUST IN THE WIND, DUDE." — TED
"DUST. WIND." — BILL
"DUDE." — TED

**Opposite:** Socrates and Bill & Ted traveling through the circuits of time.

**Top:** Socrates, Billy the Kid, Bill & Ted escape a beheading in the middle ages.

**Above:** Bill & Ted arrive in the middle ages, looking for "personages of historical significance."

# BILLY THE KID/DAN SHOR

**"HOW'S IT GOING? I'M BILLY THE KID."** — BILLY THE KID

**Opposite:** Billy the Kid (Dan Shor), Bill & Ted in the old west. Promo shot.

**Above:** Bill & Ted play poker in the old west.

**Below:** Bill & Ted in the phone booth, carefully camouflaged between two outhouses.

**Above:** Billy the Kid, Socrates, Bill & Ted arrive in Vienna with a view to rounding up Sigmund Freud.

**Below:** Billy the Kid goes down a storm in the finale/history test.

**Above:** Billy the Kid, Bill & Ted arrive in the middle ages, later to meet The Princesses.

# JOAN OF ARC/JANE WIEDLIN

"MISS OF ARC TOTALLY ROUSTED THE ENGLISH FROM FRANCE.
AND THEN SHE TURNED THIS DUDE DAUPHIN INTO A KING." — TED

Opposite (top): Joan of Arc demonstrates aerobics at the mall; (below): Meets Ted.

Left and above: Ms Of Arc's takeover of the mall demonstration earns her a police escort.

Below: Bill swordfighting with Joan of Arc.

# GENGHIS KHAN/AL LEONG

**Above:** Genghis Khan in history class from a deleted (subsequently lost) scene.

**Below:** Genghis Khan and Abraham Lincoln.

**Opposite:** Genghis Khan "totally ravaged Oshman's Sporting Goods" in the San Dimas mall.

# ABRAHAM LINCOLN/ROBERT V. BARRON

"ONE OF THE GREATEST PRESIDENTS IN AMERICAN HISTORY,
MR ABRAHAM LINCOLN!" – TED

**Top:** Abraham Lincoln is arrested by San Dimas' finest.

**Left, center:** Abraham Lincoln and Billy the Kid eat in the food court at the mall.

**Left:** Abraham Lincoln summing up at Bill & Ted's history presentation.

**Opposite:** Abraham Lincoln, shortly before an altercation with the photographer – who wants his "props" back.

# SIGMUND FREUD/ROD LOOMIS

"TED'S FATHER'S OWN FEAR OF FAILURE HAS CAUSED HIM TO MAKE HIS SON THE EMBODIMENT OF ALL OF HIS OWN DEEPEST ANXIETIES ABOUT HIMSELF. AND HENCE, HIS AGGRESSION TRANSFERS ONTO TED." — FREUD

**Opposite:** Analysis not required as Sigmund Freud helps Bill with the chores.

**Above:** Sigmund Freud and Abraham Lincoln looking serious in San Dimas.

**Below:** Sigmund Freud in an analysis session with Ted.

# RUFUS/GEORGE CARLIN

"YOU SEE, EVENTUALLY YOUR MUSIC WILL HELP PUT AN END TO WAR AND POVERTY. IT WILL ALIGN THE PLANETS AND BRING THEM INTO UNIVERSAL HARMONY, ALLOWING MEANINGFUL CONTACT WITH ALL FORMS OF LIFE, FROM EXTRATERRESTRIAL BEINGS TO COMMON HOUSEHOLD PETS. AND... IT'S EXCELLENT FOR DANCING." – RUFUS

# CAPTAIN LOGAN/HAL LANDON JR.

Left: Ted's father informs Ted in no uncertain terms that he'll be off to military school in Alaska if he fails his history test.

Above and beow: Captain Logan at work (Hal Landon Jr.).

# MISSY/AMY STOCH

Above: Missy waters her garden as the time machine lands, with Bill & Ted and the subjects for their history report.

Below: Missy offers Bill & Ted a lift home from school.

Right: Missy/Mom/Wife/Sister-in-law (Amy Stoch).

# THE PRINCESSES/DIANE FRANKLIN & KIMBERLEY LABELLE

"OH, YOU BEAUTIFUL BABES FROM ENGLAND, FOR WHOM WE HAVE TRAVELED THROUGH TIME. WILL YOU GO TO THE PROM WITH US IN SAN DIMAS? WE WILL HAVE A MOST TRIUMPHANT TIME!" — BILL & TED

"PUT THEM IN THE
IRON MAIDEN."
— EVIL DUKE

"IRON MAIDEN?
EXCELLENT!"
— BILL & TED

"EXECUTE THEM!"
— EVIL DUKE

"BOGUS!"
— BILL & TED

# CLARENCE CLEMONS, MARTHA DAVIS, FEE WAYBILL

"WELL, WE GOTTA GET BACK TO OUR REPORT..." – BILL
"...WE'D TAKE YOU WITH US BUT IT'S A HISTORY REPORT, NOT A FUTURE REPORT." – TED

**Opposite:** Travelling by accident to The Future, Bill & Ted meet their worshippers.    **Above:** Bill & Ted, with the "Three Most Importand People in the World.".

# ON LOCATION

"THIS IS THE SAN DIMAS MALL, AND THIS IS WHERE PEOPLE OF TODAY'S WORLD HANG OUT... EVERYBODY GET TOGETHER, REMEMBER WHO YOUR BUDDY IS." – BILL

# MERCHANDISE

With the cult success of the movies, merchandising kicked in full force, much of it targeting young children who loved the film. Bill & Ted Saturday morning cartoons, breakfast cereal, action figures, fan clubs, and comics cropped up. No marketing stone was left unturned.

**Top:** Coupon for Bill & ted's Most Excellent Cereal, from Ralston Purina.

**Above:** Toy Ted drives a toy car: Kenner Toys' "Talking Cruiser".

**Right:** Kenner Toys' Bill and Abe Lincoln rock out on the back of the "Boom Truck," with its portable sound stage.

**Left:** Kenner Toyschris's Phone Booth Playset.

**Right:** The Most Excellent Motorcycle, featuring Bill, Ted, and Genghis Khan (figures sold separately.)

**Left:** Bill & Ted's Excellent Adventure Jam Session Two-Pack came with "an all-new tape of six different tunes."

**Below:** Wyld Stallyns Speaker & Tape Accessory.

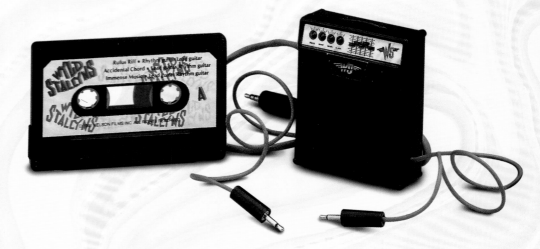

BILL AND TED'S ATTEMPTS TO OBTAIN FUTURE COPIES OF THEIR MOST EXCELLENT COMIC BOOK VIA TIME TRAVEL GO SLIGHTLY AWRY.

**Opposite:** Cover for *Bill & Ted's Most Excellent Adventures* comic book.

**Above:** The Game Boy and Atari Lynx versions of the *Bill & Ted's Excellent Adventure* videogames.

**Far left:** Pages from Bill & Ted fan mailing promoting the comics.

**Left:** Cover of Bill & Ted's fan club newsletter #2 from January 1992.

**Below:** Advertisement for mobile phone Bill & Ted game.

---

entertainment anywhere!

## Bill & Ted's Excellent Adventure

**Be excellent to each other!**

Their history report is due soon, but our **heroic dudes** have nothing to show! Can you help Bill & Ted adventure back into history to **enlist the help of some of the great names of the past**, or will you meet a fate most heinous and totally un-cool?

Guide Bill & Ted through historic landscapes to earn the trust of history's heroes. You can control either, or both characters at one time. Make sure you use their abilities to the fullest in order to solve the **fiendish puzzles** and **escape the guardians of the past**. Will history defeat you, or will the Wyld Stallions return to San Dimas triumphant?

**Features:**

- Control both Bill and Ted to adventure through history

- Choose your own path through each time zone

- Receive help and advice from Rufus and the people you meet

- Numerous side-quests to explore if you wish

**BiLL & TeD's EXCELLENT adventure**

Genre: Adventure
Available: **Q3, 2004**

Handsets: Nokia Series 30/40/60; Sharp GX10/20; Motorola T720 ... more TBA

**10**

**A**thens, Greece, 410 B.C. Bill philosophizes with Socrates, proclaiming, "All we are is dust in the wind."

**44**

**B**ill and Ted decide to really learn to play their guitars. Rufus drops by to see his excellent friends and brings them a surprise — the babes in savory clothes!

**21**

**O**rleans, France, 1429. Joan of Arc's prayer is interrupted as the phone booth drops in front of her. She joins the other historical figures.

**54**

**E**vil Bill and Ted reveal that their mission is to totally kill Bill and Ted and to take over their lives.

**28**

**M**issy meets historical figures and informs Bill his chores must be done before she will give them a ride. Everyone pitches in.

**67**

**B**ill and Ted, motioning for Beelzebub, climb off their rock onto the gargoyle's nose, then onto the base of the stairway. They ask if they can go back to San Dimas. Instead, they suddenly drop through a trapdoor.

**Above:** Bill & Ted trading cards, covering both of the first two movies.   **Below:** Bill & Ted fan club merchandise ordering brochure.   **Below:** Bill & Ted authorised clothing line.

CHECK OUT WHAT'S CURRENTLY AVAILABLE FROM

BILL & TED'S BOGUS JOURNEY © 1991 Orion Pictures Corporation. All Rights Reserved.

**BiLL & Ted's**
*OUTSTANDING*
PAST and
FUTURE
APPRECIATION SOCIETY

P.O. BOX 4769   SAN DIMAS, CA  91773   USA

JANUARY 1992 ORDERING CATALOGUE

**Opposite:** Promotional poster for *Bill & Ted's Excellent Adventure.*

Chris and Ed's original title for the second movie was *Bill & Ted Go to Hell*, and it was a much darker view of the world than what eventually made it to the screen. "I loved how audacious *Bill & Ted Go to Hell* was, and amazingly no one at the studio bumped on it," recalls Kroopf.

"To some degree *Bogus Journey* suffered from being a sequel, and in other ways it benefited," Matheson recalls. "The studio wanted to move

really, really fast and because of that I think we actually got a story across that if they'd had time to think about, they never would have done. Bill and Ted are murdered by evil versions of themselves and they go to Hell. That's amazing; I marvel at that to this day. There was another story they wanted to do at first that was just like the first film, only Bill and Ted go into literature. We didn't want to do that, and Alex and Keanu

"I'M REALLY PROUD OF HOW WEIRD AND ALMOST EXPERIMENTAL SOME OF THE JOKES ARE." — CHRIS MATHESON

LARGE EASTER BUNNY
8 FOOT Bunny

TOY BUNNY

**Opposite:** Bill & Ted costume shots for *Bill & Ted's Bogus Journey*.

**This page:** Costume, prop and vehicle polaroids for *Bill & Ted's Bogus Journey*.

didn't want to do that. We all thought it was boring. Then we had this other idea that just made us laugh. It was really weird. At that point we called it *Bill & Ted Go to Hell*, and I don't think we really thought we'd get it across. But Alex and Keanu got behind it and the studio was in a hurry. The trade-off was it wasn't fully ready. So act three's a little bit sloppy. We got something made that I don't think we would have gotten made

otherwise. I'm really proud of how weird and almost experimental some of the jokes are in that movie."

The original concept was mitigated by studio sensibilities, and the second half significantly rewritten (and toned down) from the writers' original vision. But what remained was still remarkable – who can forget Bill and Ted playing Twister with Death – and was a successful release.

**Opposite, above:** Evil Bill & Ted, De Nomolos and Rufus in the Future.

**Opposite, below:** Bill & Ted become Dead Bill & Ted, and the Wyld Stallyns van is stolen by Evil Bill & Ted.

**Above:** Bill & Ted, Station, and Death in the hardware store buying the materials they will use to make Robot Bill & Ted.

**Left:** Evil Bill & Ted in the phone booth.

**Below:** Bill & Ted rock out at the Battle of the Bands, in the finale of *Bill & Ted's Bogus Journey*.

# THE FUTURE

"NO LONGER WILL OUR FUTURE SOCIETY BE BASED ON THE IDEALS AND THE MUSIC OF THESE TWO FOOLS!"
– DE NOMOLOS

**Opposite, (top):** Rufus and the evil De Nomolos.

**Opposite, (below):** Rufus in the future.

**Left:** Statue of Bill & Ted in the future, outisde Bill & Ted University.

**Above and below:** Rufus follows the phone booth that transports Evil Bill & Ted to the present day, to find Bill & Ted and kill them.

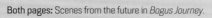

"WHAT A SHITHEAD." – JAMES MARTIN, FAITH NO MORE

# DE NOMOLOS/JOSS ACKLAND

Evil De Nomolos (Ed Solomon backwards!) is a fascist who wants to destroy the future utopia that worships Bill & Ted..

# EVIL BILL & TED

This page: Evil Bill & Ted are ruthless robots..

**Opposite (above):** Evil Bill & Ted take great pleasure in disposing of Bill & Ted, then trashing their apartment

**Opposite (below):** Evil Bill & Ted report to De Nomolos with an eye-based communiction device

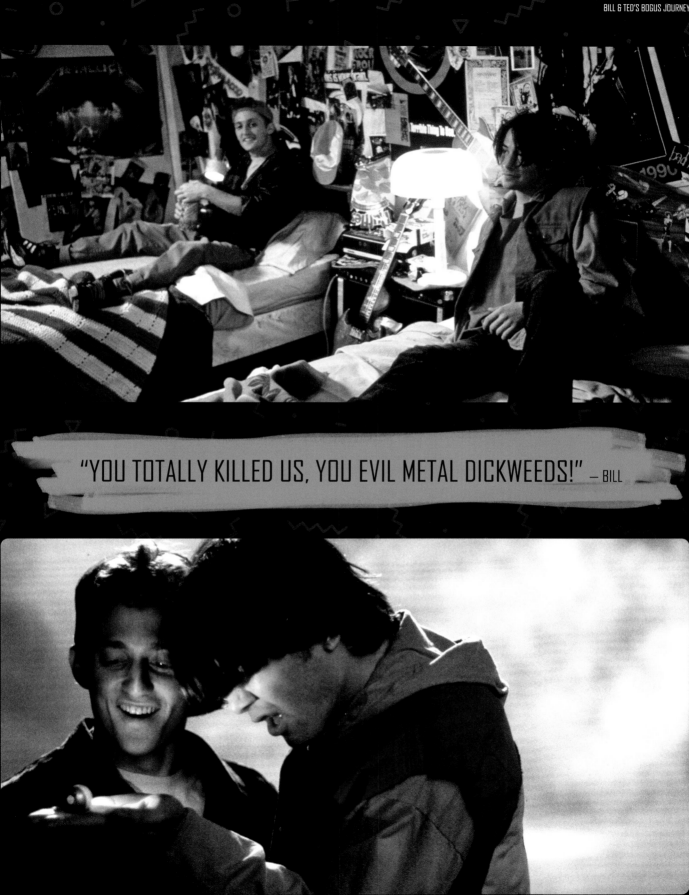

"YOU TOTALLY KILLED US, YOU EVIL METAL DICKWEEDS!" — BILL

**Above and Opposite:** Evil Bill & Ted take Bill & Ted out to the desert and kill them by throwing them from a cliff.

**Below and Left:** Evil Bill & Ted take over Bill & Ted's lives and trash their home.

# GHOST BILL & TED

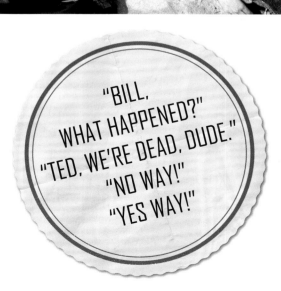

"BILL, WHAT HAPPENED?"
"TED, WE'RE DEAD, DUDE."
"NO WAY!"
"YES WAY!"

**This page:** Bill & Ted – dead in the desert – rise up as ghosts before a trip to the afterlife, Heaven and Hell.

**Opposite:** Missy holds a séance in an attempt to raise the spirit of Ty Cobb, and unwittingly sends the ghosts of Bill & Ted to Hell. Writers Chris Matheson and Ed Solomon are among the guests.

# THE SEANCE

"DOES THIS SEANCE STUFF EVER WORK?" - BILL
"NO, BUT IT WILL TODAY, DUDE." - TED

# HELL

**Above:** Bill's special Hell – Granny Preston, played with delight by Alex Winter himself.

**Below:** "A kiss, for your dear old granny..."

**Top left:** Production polaroid of Hell.

**Top right:** Colonel Oats.

**Above:** "Yes sir, sir, dude."
"Get down and give me... infinity."

**Below:** Ted's own special Hell recalls a traumatic encounter with the Easter Bunny.

"TED, IT'S THE GRIM REAPER!" "OH, HOW'S IT HANGIN', DEATH?" — BILL

**Opposite:** Bill & Ted, following their descent into the fiery pits of Hell.

**Above:** Bill & Ted challenge Death in order to get out of Hell.

**Below:** The choice of Battleship proves successful for Bill & Ted, but Death demands more: "Best three of five!"

# HEAVEN

**Opposite:** After winning all the games, Bill & Ted ascend to Heaven, taking Death (in disguise as a girl) with them.

**Top:** Special guest, legendary musician Taj Mahal, who played Heaven's Gatekeeper, alongside director Peter Hewitt.

**Top (right):** A painted set from Heaven. The staircase from *A Matter of Life and Death* (1946) was used for *Bogus Journey*.

**Above (center):** "Could you maybe help us find someone who could maybe help us build something?" Station is the answer from God.

**Above:** Death in Heaven, in a freshly stolen disguise.

**Right:** A publicity shot of the visitors in Heaven.

# STATION

"STATION! WHAT ARE YOU DOING?" — TED
"DUDE, THIS IS NO TIME TO BE PLAYING GAMES!" — BILL

**Both pages:** Multiple iterations of Station – Bill & Ted's God-given solution to being killed by Evil Bill & Ted.

# ROBOT BILL & TED

**Both pages:** Constructed by the Stations from a variety of parts from the hardware store, Robot Bill & Ted make short work of Evil Bill & Ted.

# BATTLE OF THE BANDS

**Opposite:** Present day Bill & Ted shredding at the Battle of the Bands.

**This page:** Future Rock Star Bill & Ted crushing it at the Battle of the Bands.

Decades passed. Keanu became one of the biggest stars in the world; Alex became a respected writer and director; Ed went on to write feature films and television; Chris wrote and directed several films and authored two books. Bill & Ted lived on in their hearts, and on cable, VHS, DVD, Blu-ray, and streaming. The OG fans grew up and had kids of their own, creating a new generation of Bill & Ted appreciators.

"BILL & TED ARE QUANTUM IN A WAY. THEY'RE INDIVIDUALS, BUT THEY MOVE IN THEIR OWN LITTLE KIND OF COMPLEMENTARY SPHERE. I THINK RHYTHM AND SHAPE ARE IMPORTANT TO THE CHARACTERS AND THINGS THAT ALEX AND I THINK ABOUT IN OUR PERFORMANCES."

— KEANU REEVES

"What Bill & Ted end up accessing is not different points in space and time, or even different parallel realities. They're accessing a super deep level of reality, a quantum source code. By changing their point of view, they change the source code, and the rest of reality changes to accommodate that. In the end, what they need to do to save the world is to show how all these different points of view can come together and harmonize, creating a new type of reality, built from relationships between things, not things in themselves. A world where empathy is as important as truth."

Spyridon Michalakis, Doctor of Philosophy and Applied Mathematics at the California Institute of Technology, consultant on *Bill & Ted Face the Music*.

# BILL & TED
## FACE THE MUSIC

IN 2007, TWENTY YEARS AFTER FILMING *EXCELLENT ADVENTURE*, ALEX WINTER HOSTED A BARBECUE AT HIS HOME IN LOS ANGELES WITH KEANU, CHRIS AND ED. THEY STARTED TALKING ABOUT WHERE MIDDLE-AGED BILL & TED WOULD BE IN THEIR LIVES, AND THE SEED OF *BILL & TED FACE THE MUSIC* WAS PLANTED.

"The third film was birthed at my house, with Keanu and Chris and Ed," Alex recalls. "We were shooting the breeze and talking about the characters and where they might have landed in their older age. Chris and Ed had this sketchy outline of an idea – almost looking at it like *A Christmas Carol*. Bill and Ted have not fulfilled their destiny and go on a multiverse adventure to try to figure out what went wrong and where it went wrong. We all really loved the idea, and it kind of hit us that this was actually worth trying to do."

Ed recalls the creative conversation, "What would happen if you were told as a teenager that your aspiration, and your joy – for them it was heavy metal – was going to save the world. And you were actually tasked with this. What happens if that never panned out and now you're

"DUDE, THAT TOTALLY WORKED!" — BILL
"YAH, MAYBE WE SHOULD ALWAYS NOT KNOW WHAT WE'RE DOING." — TED

**Above and Below:** Promo shots of Alex Winter and Keanu Reeves from the *Entertainment Weekly* article which helped get *Bill & Ted Face the Music* off the ground

**Opposite:** The gates of Hell.

middle-aged? How would you relieve that burden? What if you were focused so much on that you lost focus on other things in your life?

"Then we met again at my house, around 2008. We pitched around this notion that Chris and I had come up with. Chris and I both have children. We have daughters – we both have a son and daughter. And we said, 'What if it's not them? What if it's their kids? What if Rufus got the wrong Preston/Logan?' That would be a wonderful and moving way to end this series. The guys responded to that, and then Chris and I went off and started trying to come up with more notions, and more ideas, and start to form it. And then, at a certain point, Alex and Keanu said, 'yeah, that sounds good. Let's write a script.' We agreed to write it on spec (speculative, for no money up front) because we didn't want a studio trying to get us to rehash the old movies. We wanted to come up with something that the four of us felt creatively we could get behind.

"On a business level, that's one of the stupidest things you can do, to write a screenplay for a movie that you don't own or control, so you only have one outlet. (Orion had gone bankrupt by this time, and MGM had purchased the rights to the first two films, including the right to make a sequel.) So it's not like we wrote a script and then had the ability to go everywhere in town with it. We wrote a spec script that we had to bring to one place, and to convince them that there was an audience for a third film. As I remember, we had our first script around 2010."

Then this bodacious foursome embarked upon the process of actually trying to get the movie made. When they went to MGM, they found out that the studio had developed – unbeknownst to them – a reboot with young Bill & Ted. The studio didn't want to do Bill and Ted as middle-aged men, and even Keanu's prodigious box office potential wasn't enough to convince them. Because there was no

**Opposite:** Babe Ruth, in the middle of hitting a home run, replaces George Washington crossing the Delaware.

**Below:** Rufus' watch from the future, counting down to the end of the world.

foreign theatrical release for either of the first two films, there were no foreign box office numbers to justify international financing and distribution. Projections based on international distribution are crucial to getting a film greenlit, and those projections are based on what came before. The number crunchers didn't have their usual data and said it was not worth the risk. There was no way acceptable to the business side of the industry to quantify the way the movie had grown culturally over 30 years – it was anecdotal. "When I would travel to a conference," Ed recalls, "or to give a lecture, or talk to a film school – I'm talking about in Beirut, or Seoul, or in Europe, anywhere – the movie that always generated the biggest response was the idea of a third Bill & Ted movie. I'm talking bigger than *Men in Black*, bigger than anything I've worked on. But there were no numbers to justify that, so it became me and Chris and Alex and Keanu, saying, 'we really believe, from our experience, that there's an audience for this.'"

Around 2013, they brought in Dean Parisot, best known as the director of *Galaxy Quest*, a film with a similar comedic sensibility and a loyal fanbase. "The reason we brought this movie to Dean Parisot," Ed recalls, "was that we know Dean well, creatively and personally. He made *Galaxy Quest*, one of the best comedies of the 2000s. He's a good-hearted man who also has suffered a fair amount of loss in his life, and he could really relate to the underlying ideas. There's a sadness

and disappointment at the core of the comedy of this movie."

Dean remembers going to Keanu's house at some point in the long, long development process: "I said, 'Well, you know, you guys have been on this for, like, nine years.' He says, 'Dude, *you've* been on it for six!' I didn't even realize I'd been on for that long. We'd gone through so many companies trying to get it set up. So when we did get it set up, we realized we had no money at all, really, to make something. It's fine to make a movie, let's say, like *Green Book*. The actual physical part of it is two guys in the car. So you need a car, and a couple of houses someplace. This movie takes place in the past, in the future, in Hell, in the structure of all space and time. It has a killer robot and prosthetic makeup. Those things don't exist unless you create them, and we had no money to create any of them. We had no money at first even to have production offices; so my house was the production office. For months, I'd walk downstairs after getting my coffee, and everyone was there, and we would go to work, and then I would finish the day, have some supper, go upstairs and go to sleep. It's very odd to have a production company in your dining room every day. I've been calling us 'the band.' The band stayed together to make this movie. We had an affection for each other, and we're all after the same thing together, and we don't have enough to pull this off. So we're trying to figure out how to pull it off and not spend anything."

The "band" persevered, along with Scott Kroopf, producer of the first two films, who volunteered to produce *Face the Music*. They spent years negotiating with MGM, putting together financing deals that went south when executives shifted, and rewriting the script numerous times. Kroopf credits some well-timed press for turning up the heat: "Alex Winter knew someone at *Entertainment Weekly*, and they decided to do a Bill & Ted reunion article. It got an unbelievable amount of attention, and suddenly everyone was saying, 'Maybe there is something there?' Keanu introduced us to Scott Fisher, who introduced us to Alex Lebovici and Steve Ponce, and their company Hammerstone Studios." Hammerstone agreed to fully finance the film, and Keanu and Alex Winter filmed an announcement at the Hollywood Bowl, generating a YouTube video that got tens of millions of hits, and *Bill & Ted Face the Music* became a top 5 trending film across all domestic social media platforms in 2019.

After – literally – years of discussion, MGM agreed to let them make the film, which they would distribute under the newly re-launched Orion label.

Chris Matheson has a simpler analysis. "It's completely simple: it anguished, it languished, it languished. *John Wick* happened. Boom. That's it. Who would be dumb enough to not spend some money to see Keanu Reeves play Ted again after *John Wick 3*? It was going to happen at that point."

Hammerstone made a deal with MGM and raised the money. Alex Lebovici credits the confluence of events, "The spring and summer of 2019 was The Keanaissance! John Wick 3, Toy Story 4, and the announcement of Bill & Ted Face the Music all came together in the public consciousness right around the time we were preparing to go to the international market at Cannes. Because of that there was a justification to reimagine the size and scale of the film; the budget increased 33%, and we were able to make the film even bigger and more exciting."

But then, at the last minute, as they were in the final days of pre-production, some of the money got cold feet. Ed recalls that week as stressful: "We lost half our financing two weeks before we were set to start shooting. Even though the people who put the money in were incredibly generous, we still didn't have the budget we needed. Ultimately, two men, Patrick Dugan and David Haring, stepped up. We owe our financial survival to those guys. I have never been involved in a production that's been – on a production level – this stressful, but once it was up and running, had such joy and jovial spirit on the set. It really was an incredible experience creatively, although on a production level an incredibly stressful one."

"There are ten other small investors in the movie." says Alex Leibovici

"SOMETIMES THINGS DON'T MAKE SENSE UNTIL THE END OF THE STORY." — RUFUS

**Above:** Director Dean Parisot working with Keanu Reeves, Alex Winter and Kid Cudi.

**Opposite:** The last supper, Bill & Ted style.

"Hammerstone's friends and family kept the project on track until David and Patrick stepped in to help save the day. When they came in, they also let all the early friends and family continue to participate in the film. Every one of the investors is a fan. Everyone on the crew is a fan."

Even the weather plagued them, Alex Winter recalls, "We got hit by a hurricane on week three. The whole time we were in New Orleans it was either hurricanes or flash floods or 115-degree weather."

The intrepid filmmakers persevered; the project was saved time and time again by the good will – the excellence – of the team and the people around them.

"We knew it was only going to be made with a group of people who had an affection for the movie and who we all had affection for," Dean recalls. "The thing that was so great about making the movie is that we all wanted to. We just wanted to see if we could pull it off. A lot of us have been in the business for a long time. It wasn't about how much money we were making; I think we gave half of it back before we started. That goodwill, it starts with Keanu and Alex, who have tremendous goodwill toward each other. And then Chris and Ed and Scott, and then I sort of

joined the band later. Everyone just kept staying as things were blowing up around us – it was 100 degrees, 100 per cent humidity, we only had one robot costume, we only had one of everything.

"I was able to bring in a group of people I've worked with over many, many years who all just said 'We don't care what happens. We're just gonna keep making this until someone tells us to go home.'

"It also happened in New Orleans. People were like, 'No way. Bill and Ted? We'll be there!' It was odd, and great.

"Be excellent to each other. Yeah, that's why everybody showed up. And that's why everybody refused to leave and did everything they could. Everyone was on the same train together. That's the thing you're trying to do is get everybody moving together."

"It was this great family environment," Alex remembers. "Dean has this great attitude on set. We were working really, really, really hard, and it's really, really, really physical. I remember at the end of week one, we were having a lot of fun. Everyone was laughing a lot, and we felt like the film was off to a good start. But Keanu and I looked at each other and he was like, 'This is harder than the first two right?' I was like, 'Yeah, this is. Definitely.' He's like, 'It's not just because we're old, right?' He had just finished *John Wick 3*, which is sort of like doing a high wire act for Barnum & Bailey, and was on his way to *Matrix 4*. I'm in really good shape. I'm actually probably in better physical shape now than I was then. But it was frickin hard! We just looked at each other and were like, 'This is going to be hard. We've got to make sure we get our rest. We've got to make sure we eat right.' And that's really what we did. We tucked in. We worked seven days a week, he and I. We would shoot five days and then we would work together, usually both days of the weekend, on the scenes that we had coming up. There was a lot of physical prep work that we needed to do. We were very much in the trenches together for those months that we were shooting."

Ed credits Alex and Keanu: "They showed up every day incredibly prepared, ready to work, having deeply studied their roles, having everything memorized, knowing that we were shooting fast because we didn't have a lot of days to shoot. Everything emanates outward from that. I think Alex Winter's performance is revelatory. He had been directing movies and changed paths in his career, but he put the work in to bring himself to a place where he was able to not just step up and do it, but to really, really shine. And I think the two of them had each other's back in the process because they're very good friends, and that really comes out. From the beginning to the end of the process, the guys were really there for each other as well as the rest of us. It set the tone for why the creative experience was so joyful and delightful. It was hard work. People worked really hard, but there's a joy in that. there's a joy in working hard when you're all working toward a common goal."

**Opposite:** Bill & Ted – and friends – return to Hell in *Bill & Ted Face the Music*.

**Above:** Director Dean Parisot in front of set inspiration and photography.

**Below:** *Bill and Ted Face the Music* mood boards.

# BE EXCELLENT TO EACH OTHER...

"Be excellent to each other" has become the thematic spine of the world of Bill & Ted. "When we were first writing the script," Ed Solomon recalls, "We thought, what if Rufus, instead of being a 27-year-old high school sophomore, is an emissary from the future who brings them to the future where they're potentially dressed down. Then we started laughing at the idea that when they show up in the future, they're viewed as God, which, compared to them as high school students who couldn't even get dates, seemed funny to us. Then, we said, 'Okay, when the people in the future ask them to say something wise, what would they say?' Without any hesitation – I don't remember if it was Chris or me – said 'Be excellent to each other!' And the other one said, 'And party on, dudes!' We just laughed and we kept going; we didn't think twice about it. We didn't think about it as being an important line. We certainly never expected that during this horrible Coronavirus Pandemic that suddenly it would be on hundreds of marquees of closed movie theaters throughout the country. And we, of course, never thought would have any social relevance because we didn't even think people were going to read the screenplay, let alone that it would be made into a movie. We had no idea. But it emanated purely out of the spirit of the characters that Chris and I so loved inhabiting, a kind of benign joyfulness in the sense that every human being on the planet was equivalent."

"Be Excellent To Each Other," Alex says, "is at once odd and perfectly relatable. So it gives you pause, makes you sit up and listen a little and at the same time it's light and not grandiose. But mostly I love it because it's actionable, it's asking us all to do something that's simple and beautiful. It's not saying we should be perfect or saint-like or 'better than', just that we should take the action of being our better selves to those around us. And that's something we could all benefit from in these very stressful times."

The San Dimas version of the golden rule includes its own very important coda...

**Opposite:** Greenscreen shots of Bill & Ted in the future.

**Below:** Kid Cudi on stage with Thea & Billie and the Greatest Musicians Who Ever Lived.

# ...AND PARTY ON, DUDES!

"...And Party on!" Keanu adds. "It's a profound statement. Do the best of yourself. Treat each other with kindness, respect, with love, with appreciation. It's like, all the good things, all the good stuff. Be excellent to each other. It's a wonderful sentiment. It's one of the best, right? Yeah, and it feels good. It feels good to be excellent to people! It feels great to be treated excellently. It's the gold standard for our humanity, our humanness, our connection to everything."

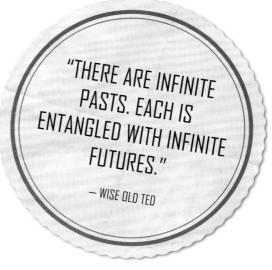

"THERE ARE INFINITE PASTS. EACH IS ENTANGLED WITH INFINITE FUTURES."

— WISE OLD TED

# BILL S. PRESTON, ESQ./ALEX WINTER
# THEODORE "TED" LOGAN/KEANU REEVES

"The casting process was a long process. I probably saw about 150, 200 kids," recalls Stephen Herek. "I started to learn something about how the lines were being said, and what the attitude of Bill and Ted should be. It wasn't until about week two of actual shooting that I realized—because I had a dog who was a puppy at the time—that it was the unabashed, unconditional love and excitement for life that puppies have. A light bulb went on in my head. It was like, "This is what I want from Bill and Ted. This incredible effusive nature. I said, "What I want

is like you guys to be Labrador retriever puppies", I distilled it down to "I need more puppy factor." They immediately got what I was talking about. That's the spirit that I wanted from these two characters. I was a big giant puppy as well, throughout all of this."

"I always thought Bill & Ted had a lot of energy," Keanu says. "A youthful kind of innocence to them. They also had a kind of fortitude and inventiveness."

**Opposite:** Bill & Ted just before playing "The Song That Saves The World."

**Above:** Bill & Ted play at Missy and Deacon's wedding.

**Below:** Bill & Ted race to the trusty phone booth, trying to find the song.

"Alex and I became fast friends during the audition process of the first film," continued Keanu. "We had a lot in common. We shared a similar humor, and just creatively we connected. Talking about the characters as commedia dell'arte. To have that kind of a conversation about Bill and Ted in the beginning was like, "Oh, okay. We get this. We get each other. We made each other laugh, and enjoyed working together. We became friends after working together, and have worked together on projects outside of Bill and Ted. It was a real joy to work with him again and spend time together like that."

"This notion of the sincerity of it was something that Keanu and I had found separately in our approach to the script, that then really clicked when we did it together." Alex remembers. "Neither of us looked at these

guys in an arch way. We both had grown up doing a lot of theater, a lot of physical theater, and I think we both approached these guys in a similar way, which was to just sort of build them like you would a theatrical character, from the inside out. We didn't view the characters as broad, we viewed them as people who really experienced their world in this way, legitimately. He and I bonded over that. We have fun performing together because we have a very like-minded approach to acting and to these characters specifically. It made the playground of making the film that much more fun for everybody."

"There's a duality between the friendship between Chris and Ed and the friendship between me and Keanu. They came at these characters through their friendship and their like-minded ideas about performing and about character and about comedy. I think it's no accident that the third film came out of a conversation between the four of us that was very casual and very friendly. In a way, it was a genuine full circle."

Bill and Ted grow from teenagers to (relatively) mature adults through the three films. "It was a really cool thing about this, even the development of the characters – they start playing different versions of themselves from the second film on," Keanu observes. "They play three versions of themselves in the second film. There's Bill & Ted, Evil Bill & Ted, Robot Bill & Ted, Dead Bill & Ted. This kind of bifurcation or splitting up of the different faces or characteristics of the characters has been a lot of fun to play. And in *Face the Music* we get to play even more versions of ourselves, which is a lot of fun.

"I think they tackled all the challenges that came to them in the first two films in a youthful manner. Even in the second film, it starts to mature. I guess we could look back on these films as the developmental stages of life. They're not quite puppies anymore, thirty years later. They've got families and different responsibilities. But the music, I guess they've gone down a path that, has led them astray from the rock. Maybe they get their rock back. And their families."

**Opposite (above):** Ed Solomon and Chris Matheson as "Stupid Waiter" and "Ugly Waiter" in *Bill & Ted's Excellent Adventure.*

**Opposite (below):** Ed Solomon and Chris Matheson at the séance in *Bill & Ted's Bogus Journey,*

**Below:** Ed Solomon and Chris Matheson as demons in *Bill & Ted Face the Music.*

# KELLY/KRISTEN SCHAAL

George Carlin died in 2008, leaving his daughter Kelly to uphold his legacy, which she does with great pride and love.

Talking about *Bill & Ted's Excellent Adventure*, "Those scenes with Rufus that bookend the movie were actually written mostly by George Carlin, those jokes and stuff," Ed recalls. "George was the only person in the movie that anyone had even heard of. He was one of my idols. In fact, it might have been the first of my idols. The first comedy records I ever bought were his – I listened to him religiously."

"He was part idealist who had been heartbroken," his daughter Kelly says. "The George Carlin on the stage, he was using theatrics and language and comedy to express himself. How he treated people was very much "be excellent to each other" when he met people one-on-one, whether it was a fan, or a homeless person on the street. He was an extremely attentive, generous human being. He made a point to know every single crew person's name, and to treat them like equals. He never played the hierarchy card. My dad loved playing Rufus. He loved the character. He loved the mission. And he loved being the mentor, teacher, wise guy. He loved that role."

The character of Rufus's daughter Kelly (played by Kristen Schaal), is named after Kelly Carlin. She too is upholding her father's legacy.

**Left:** Kristen Schaal as Kelly, Rufus' daughter in *Bill & Ted Face the Music*.

**Above:** George Carlin as Rufus.

**Opposite:** Billie, Thea and Kid Cudi;

**Opposite, Inset:** Kid Cudi's special edition sneakers.

# KID CUDI

Kid Cudi plays a Bill & Ted-world version of himself, pulled around through space and time (and going to Hell) with graceful aplomb. "When we were shooting, at first I was asking, 'Is he scared? What's going through his mind?' And Dean kept saying, 'You're cool with this. You're just going with the flow.' So, I just know what this is. It's just some time travel, some quantum physics, and I'm a professional and I can figure this out.

"I chased this role down." Kid Cudi explains. "I first watched the Bill & Ted movies when I was seven years old, and they've been ingrained into my life. Bill & Ted for me are style icons. I have this deal with Adidas, and I'd already told them that I wanted to do a retro version of the shoes Bill & Ted wore in Bogus Journey, with some type of Bill & Ted merch to go

with it. I sent the producers what we'd been working on, and they loved it. Adidas was able to make me three pairs in time for the shoot. I was able to get a jacket from my good friend Don C. He did a custom version of a jacket he'd already designed, but he put my name on the back. He made it just for this movie, and I had that with the sneakers. It all came together.

"Be excellent to each other" has been my mantra since I first heard it, so that's how I live my life. I send these messages to the lost and the broken out there in the world who need someone to talk to, who need someone that understands them. So if anybody feels like music can save the world, it's me. How can we help people? How can we build people up? I know what it was like being young and not having anything to listen to that connected with me fully. Music is a tool to fix the soul."

"THERE'S NO SUCH THING AS PRESENT, PAST, FUTURE. TO REALLY DIG THE GROOVE OF THE QUANTUM REALM, YOU GOTTA CHOOSE A PLACE TO DIG IT FROM... DIG?" — KID CUDI

**Above:** Chief Chet Logan plays backup clarinet to Bill & Ted in the finale of *Bill & Ted Face the Music*.

**Below and Opposite:** Ted possess his father in *Bill & Ted's Bogus Journey*.

# CHIEF CHET LOGAN/HAL LANDON, JR.

Ted's dad, Police Chief of San Dimas, was the villain of *Excellent Adventure*, threatening Ted with exile to military school in Alaska if he fails his history exam. Veteran character actor Hal Landon, Jr. brings a depth to the character that expands through the three films.

In the second film, he's married to the beautiful Missy and enjoying his life, despite disappointment in his son. Landon displays most excellent physical comedy in the scene where Ted takes over his father's body, aptly mimicking Ted's physical looseness.

In *Face the Music*, Chet has to face the nightmare of his younger son, Deacon, marrying Missy, his now ex-wife. By the third movie, he knew the character so well he made up a detailed backstory: "Deacon says he blames me because I dumped his mother, when in fact, his mother actually left me for her tennis pro. But I let it be

known that I dumped her because I didn't want people to think that a woman would run out on me. So I was a single parent, stuck with these two boys. I had ambitions. Being Chief of Police of San Dimas was a stepping stone to larger cities and more, but all that gets ruined. First by Ted, embarrassing me with these wild, crazy claims of going into the past and the future and Heaven and Hell. He had some success as a rock musician, but because of his weirdness, that dissipates, and he's still an embarrassment. Then Deacon, the "good" son who has followed in my footsteps, marries my ex-wife, and that's the end of it for me. I know that I'll never achieve anything." By the end of *Face the Music*, Chet has been to Hell and back – literally – and has realized Ted was telling the truth all along – and the family is healed.

# MISSY PRESTON-LOGAN-LOGAN/AMY STOCH

Amy Stoch plays Missy, the cheerleader who first becomes Bill's stepmother, then Ted's stepmother and finally Ted's sister-in-law, bringing more to the role than just the typical dumb blonde.

"Yeah, she's a bombshell and everybody talks about her. But she's got the life she says she wants, she's got the husband with a great job and a nice house and the child who's already raised by somebody else. To play her as anything but a real person would do her a disservice."

In *Bogus Journey*, Missy hilariously leads a séance, trying to contact Ty Cobb, and unknowingly sends her stepsons to Hell, but she's still hot and she still cares about them. Other participants in the séance include Chris Matheson and Ed Solomon, along with a few other screenwriting friends of theirs moonlighting as actors. "Out of all of the scenes in all three films, the séance is my favorite simply because I got to do so much. It was a hysterical scene to shoot. We had a blast."

Missy has finally found her match in *Face the Music* – Ted's younger brother Deacon, now a cop working with his father. Stoch was initially uncomfortable with the idea of Missy marrying someone half her age – Missy has always been into older guys – but warmed to the idea, and generates great chemistry with Beck Bennett, who plays the grown-up Deacon. "When I knew I had to finally kiss him, I was like, 'I have to kiss someone my son's age. How can I do this?' It turned out to be so funny, with Hal in the background – oh my God – his facial expressions. Right before they yelled 'Action,' I turned to Beck and said, 'I deeply apologize for what I'm about to do to you!' and then let go! Once you let go and you got a guy who's willing to let you, and go right along with you, then that's just tremendous."

**Opposite (top):** Missy with her third husband, Ted's little brother Deacon, played by Beck Bennett from *Saturday Night Live*.

**Opposite left** and **right:** Missy with her first two husbands: Bill's dad, (left) and Ted's dad.

**Below:** Missy makes snacks for Bill & Ted, in *Excellent Adventure*.

# DEATH/WILLIAM SADLER

William Sadler has had a long and varied career, but he will probably always be remembered for his hilarious turn as Death in *Bogus Journey* and *Face the Music*. "The thing that I really liked about the character was that he starts out frightening, sinister – a really scary figure. So there's real jeopardy for the boys; they're going to stay in Hell forever if they screw this up. Then when he starts to lose the games, little by little, he gets broken down, and this other side of him, this petulant, sore loser, starts to surface. And lo and behold, he's like all of us. When he goes up to Heaven with Bill and Ted, he's embarrassed. He gets caught up in this journey, and by the end of it he wants to be one of the guys so bad. That's when I started adding things like, 'What about my butt?' He wants to be part of the band, he wants to be accepted, just like all of us, you know? I found that character arc, just really, really fun to play. In *Face the Music*, he's still that same needy person that we all are.

"One of the things that I had the most fun with playing in *Bogus Journey* was that once I was in character, once I put on the robes and the makeup and the accent – I couldn't shut him up. Everything was fair game. I would follow through on actions that were not in the script and it was just really, really fun. It was a creative playground for me. I would come up with this and that and if everybody on the set laughed, it got in the movie.

"There's a scene [in *Bogus Journey*] in the hardware store where Death sees a guy smoking and as he walks by, he says, 'See you real soon,' and the guy puts the cigarette out. That was an idea I had on set the night we were shooting and I told Peter Hewitt, the director, and he liked it, but we didn't have an actor. So he said, 'Bring the camera over here' and we shot it with him playing the guy. I love that flexibility.

"The characters of Bill and Ted are like all of us. I think what makes them so lovable is that even though they're sort of idiots about lots of things, at the bottom of it their spirit is always so buoyant and life-affirming. They're just sort of joyous fools. We see ourselves in these characters. What's fun about *Bogus Journey* is that they confront the most dire situations, their own death, with the same silliness, with the same, 'Dude, we got to do something.' 'And save the Babes.' There's something just wonderful about that genuine silliness."

**Below:** Death confronts Bill & Ted in *Face the Music*.

**Opposite Above:** Lonely Death plays tetherball with himself in Hell, green screen version.

**Opposite Below:** Dean Parisot consults with Death (William Sadler).

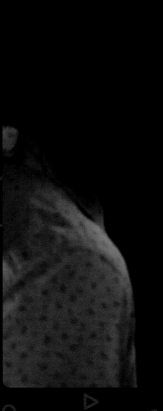

"YOU MIGHT BE A KING OR A LITTLE STREET SWEEPER, BUT SOONER OR LATER YOU DANCE WITH THE REAPER"

# PRINCESS JOANNA PRESTON/JAYMA MAYS

The Princesses have been played by different actresses in all three films: In *Excellent Adventure*, it was Diane Franklin (Joanna) and Kimberly Kates (Elizabeth); in *Bogus Journey* by Sarah Trigger (Joanna) and Annette Azcuy (Elizabeth); and in *Face the Music*, by Jayma Mays (Joanna) and Erinn Hayes (Elizabeth).

They've come a long way from escaping medieval England and marriage to some royal ugly dudes to come to 1980s San Dimas to be with their true loves, Bill & Ted. They survived the trauma of losing their beloveds in *Bogus Journey*, and now are mature bread-winners – troubled wives and moms in *Face the Music*.

**Right:** Bill & Ted charm the Princesses in *Excellent Adventure*.

**Below:** Joanna and Elizabeth in the time traveling phone booth.

**Opposite (above):** Joanna & Elizabeth grieve their dead boyfriends in *Bogus Journey*.

**Opposite: (Below):** Joanna and Elizabeth at the marriage counselor's office.

# PRINCESS ELIZABETH LOGAN/ERINN HAYES

Princess Joanna is played by Jayma Mays, known for her work on *Glee*, *Heroes*, *Ugly Betty* and *Drunk History*, and Princess Elizabeth is played by Erinn Hayes, known for the role of Dr. Lola Spratt in the satirical comedy series *Childrens Hospital* on Adult Swim, as well as *The Dangerous Book for Boys* and *Kevin Can Wait*.

Princess Joanna Preston and Princess Elizabeth Logan have just about had enough of their husbands. They love them, but the life they're living isn't working. Their desire to fix the relationships takes them to couples therapy, which has little effect after they freak out their therapist, telling her that Joanna was born in 1410, Elizabeth in 1408. They then embark upon an off-screen journey with their 93-year-old selves to try to figure out what's worth saving in their marriages to Bill & Ted, eventually coming to believe in their husbands (and daughters) once again.

# BILLIE LOGAN/BRIGETTE LUNDY-PAINE

"I didn't know the Bill and Ted movies before I auditioned, and it was just the most exciting thing to step into when I realized that it's this really beloved world, not just a movie, but this whole culture around Bill and Ted.; these gentle creatures who brought joy to so many people. It was exciting to be welcomed so fully into that world, and to have these characters who get to be Bill and Ted-esque, who Sam and I were totally given permission to make our own. It's just absolute pure love that all of the characters have for one another, but particularly the daughters and the fathers. Their family, along with the Princesses, love each other so fully and who are so lacking in judgment. Sam and I took a long time figuring out who the daughters were, how we carried on the physical and vocal comedy of Bill and Ted. How they've grown up, almost in the shadow of these – these – gods to them. How they've crafted their lives around trying to be like them, but also trying to lead in their own way." Brigitte Lundy-Paine.

**Left:** Brigette Lundy-Paine as Billie Logan.

**Above:** Dean Parisot directs Brigette Lundy-Paine and Samara Weaving.

**Below:** Daughters Thea and Bille with Death in the finale.

# THEA PRESTON/SAMARA WEAVING

"I think the great thing about Bill and Ted is that they always see the world in a positive light. They give everybody the benefit of the doubt and I think their daughters share that same outlook on life. They have this sort of profound bravery that they're oblivious too. When they're faced with a very difficult situation, they're actually very good problem solvers, which I think is a result of the blind trust they have in the universe. Billie and Thea have that same attitude and as a result they have a very deep bond with their fathers.

However, the daughters are a little bit more aware, maybe a touch more intelligent. They would do anything to help their fathers and as a result have their own brilliantly fun Bill and Ted adventure. It was a pleasure working on this project. It was just like watching the first two films: chaotic, non-sensical and a whirlwind of joy." Samara Weaving.

**Above:** Brigette Lundy-Paine and Samara Weaving.

**Right:** Samara Weaving as Thea Preston.

**Below:** Thea and Billie eavesdrop on their fathers.

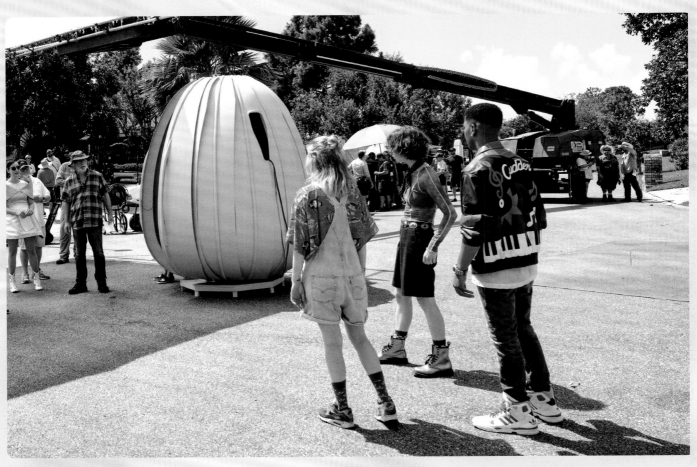

**Above:** Dean Parisot directs the Musicians, along with Bille & Thea and Kid Cudi.

**Below:** Missy with her new husband, Deacon. Ted's brother becomes his father-in-law.

**Below:** Bill, Ted, Billie and Thea.

# FATHERS AND DAUGHTERS

"When we wrote the first two movies," Ed Solomon recalls, "Chris and I were essentially adolescent boys. We were in our early 20s when we came up with the characters, and we were immature 20s at that. Of course the fantasy of an adolescent boy was that your rock band would save the world. We weren't that much more mature when we wrote the second movie. And so, of course, when Bill and Ted had kids, they'd be mini-mes—Little Bill and Little Ted. We loved the idea that Ted names his son Bill and Bill names his son Ted. Then we grew up. We had kids, we had disappointments, we suffered losses and—as life does to people—it grew us up.

"When we were first writing the script for *Face the Music*, we struggled writing Little Bill and Little Ted. It was always bad and it never satisfied us. Part of it was because we did Bill and Ted as young men; they were called Bill and Ted. We felt like we were repeating ourselves

creatively. We knew that our movie was very boyish, very male centric. What if it was daughters? What if it was Billie and Thea? And what if that's what they meant all along? Suddenly the movie opened itself up to us. The characters opened themselves up and the movie opened itself up. It rounded out. I know there are people on the Internet who think we did it for some PC reason. That's not true at all. We got a lot wrong with the first two movies. There are a lot of things we would have done better. One of them was balancing it more, in terms of gender. We just didn't know better.

"I remember when George Carlin was on the set of the first movie, we talked a lot about his daughter Kelly and he introduced me to her. We became friendly. Chris and I have daughters. Dean has a daughter. Scott Kroopf has daughters. It made sense to us that the emissary from the future would be Rufus's daughter. And that's why we named her Kelly."

"HOW YOU DOIN'?"– BILL  "WELL, YOU KNOW, WE'RE DEAD."– THEA  "AND IN HELL."– BILLIE,  "BUT HOW YOU DOIN'?"– TED  "WE'RE GOOD."– BILLIE/THEA

# THE ROBOT AKA DENNIS/ANTHONY CARRIGAN

Anthony Carrigan, best known for his roles on the TV shows *Gotham* and *Barry* (he was Emmy-nominated for his role as Noho Hank), plays The Robot, a.k.a. Dennis McCoy. He has been a Bill & Ted fan since childhood. "I was obsessed with those movies," he says. "I even tried to time travel in numerous phone booths, to no avail. I thought they were so fun and goofy and brilliant. The second film is genuinely scary. I mean, Alex Winter as his grandma is legitimately one of the most terrifying things I think I've ever seen."

"I originally based the future buildings on the work of architect Santiago Calatrava," says Dean Parisot, "and I wanted The Robot to be in that style. I wanted it to be a threatening, horrible killer robot that you think is truly going to kill Bill & Ted – and then allow it to transition. That was difficult, and it really is a credit to both Steve Wang, the designer of the suit, and Anthony. To this day. I don't know what Anthony did, but he's so physical as an actor. The first scene we shot with him was in the garage when he shoots The Great Leader's daughter and the girls and everybody goes to Hell. That first moment when he kills them, that was the first time we went, 'He is incredible, it's gonna be hysterical!' He's able to have so much riding on the fact that he needs to be great at his job, accomplish this tough-ass thing, and as he gets more and more human, things get worse and worse for him. There's one moment that we laugh about all the time, the moment where he realizes they have the song, that he's killed all of their families and lasered them to Hell. Every time we just crack up. It's a combination of his instinct as an actor, and that he also must have practiced. He wouldn't admit to it, but he must have practiced in front of a mirror. He's brilliant at improv, and we tried different things.

**Opposite (top):** Dean Parisot and Ed Solomon talk with Anthony Carrigan on set.

**Opposite (center left):** Dean Parisot directs The Robot in the prison yard scene.

**Opposite (center right and below):** Bill & Ted confront The Robot.

**Below:** Anthony Carrigan as The Robot (aka Dennis).

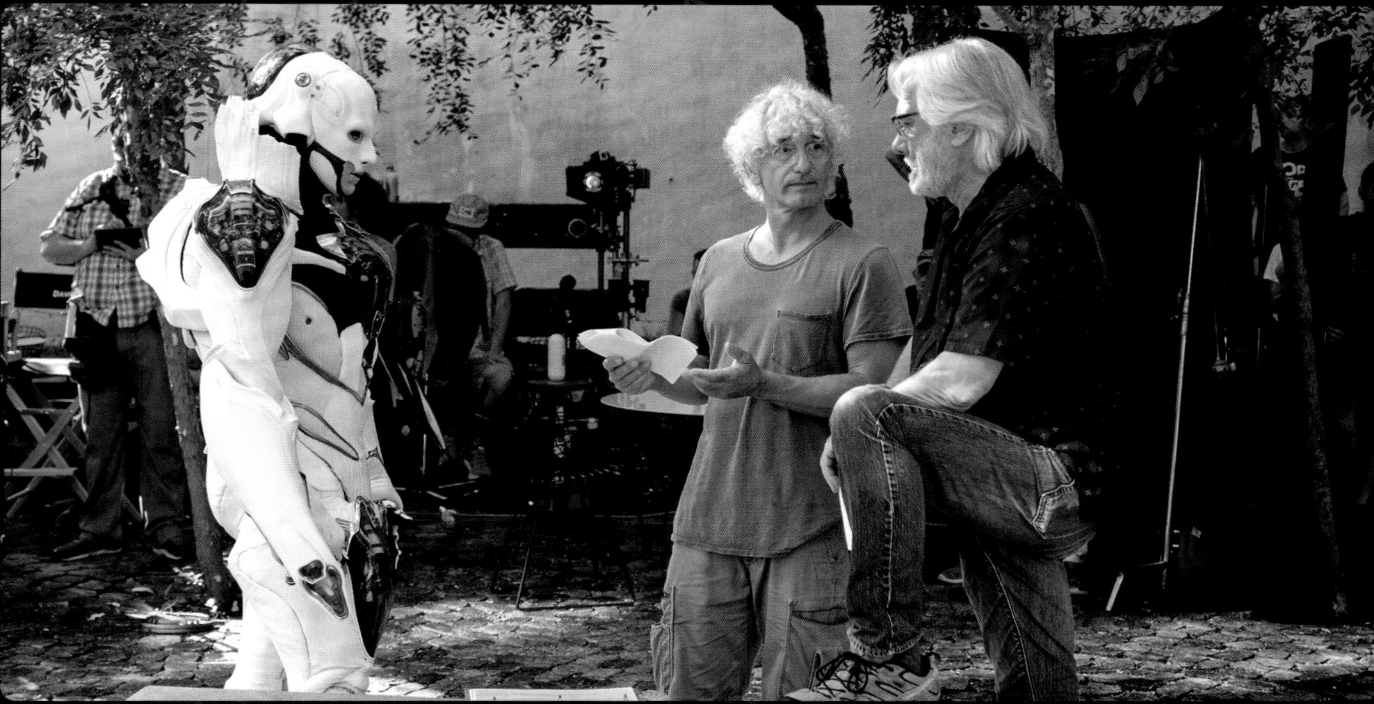

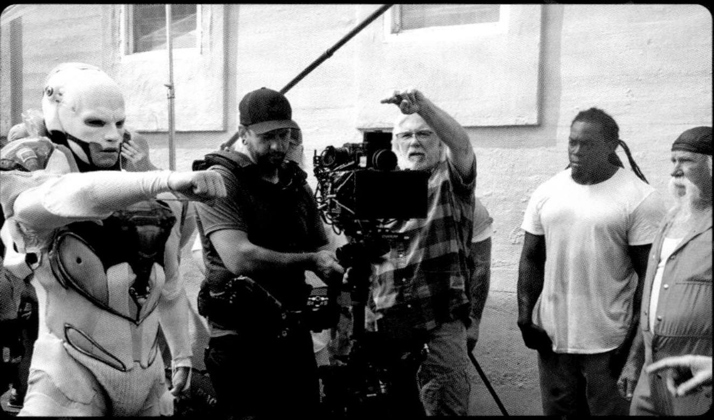

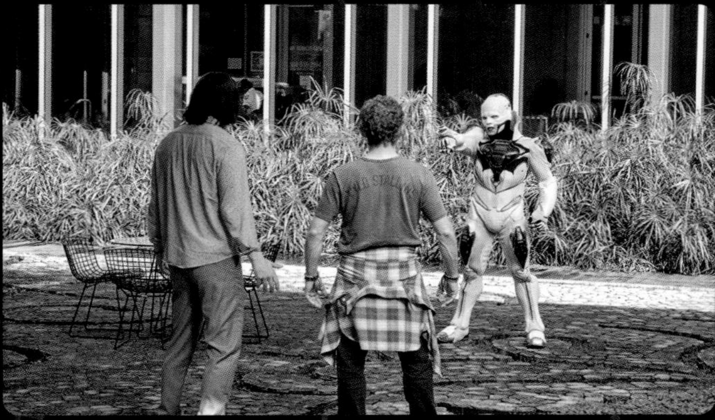

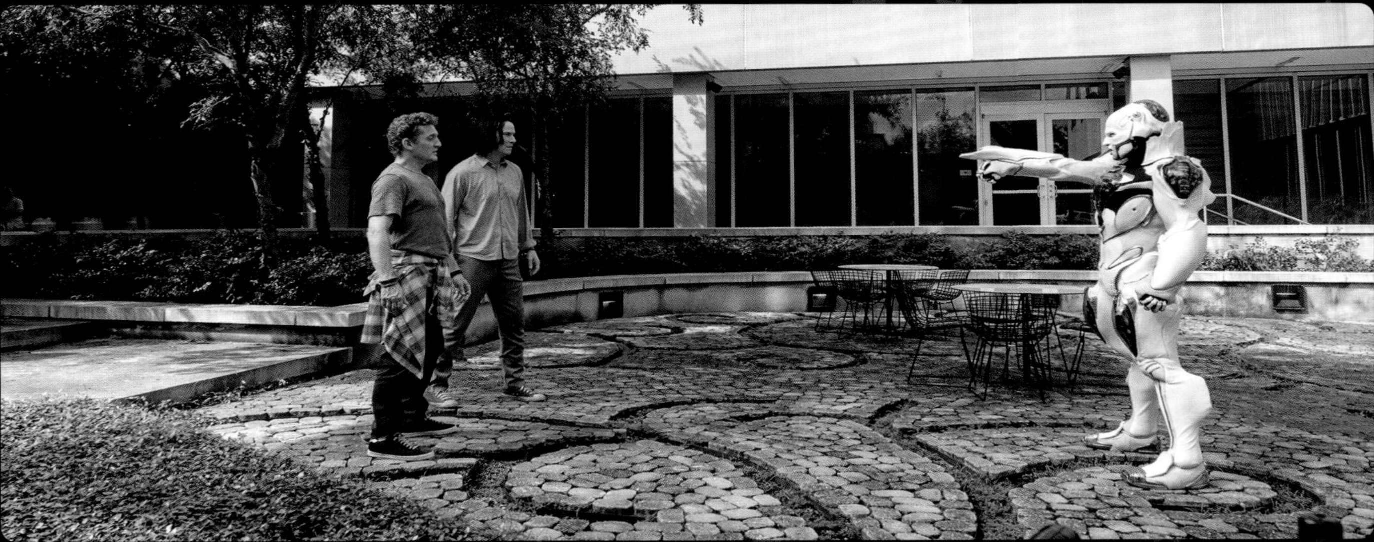

The idea is there and most of the dialogue, but there's a lot that's just him improvising."

Due to the short timeline and limited funds, the costume ended up an inch too short for Carrigan. They were told he was 5' 11" but he's really six foot. This created some discomfort: "What can I say, I'm a masochist," Anthony says. "I noticed that when I put the suit on and we did the whole thing, the makeup and everything – first of all, it looked incredible, so I didn't really want to mess with it at all. It was very constrictive, and I thought, this might really pose a challenge. But actually, when I thought about it with the character, it made total sense that this character is essentially born into the wrong body and is working against his mechanical nature to try and be more human. So it actually worked out quite well to be trying to convey emotion through a face that literally cannot move. In the New Orleans heat, it was pretty difficult. But again, I think it also informs my performance and working against all those things actually helped me find the physicality as well. He's very uncomfortable in his own skin. So, just added a bunch of discomfort, and do I need to act? I don't know."

"But that is the idea behind all of this," Dean says. "Obstacles are what you want. Really smart actors use those obstacles. Anything in his way became like gold for him. It's just great. He's got all this horrible stuff in his eyes, but he figured out how to use that. The poor bastard was in that 40 pounds of crap in the middle of summer, and he stayed on the set the whole time. Never said a word, not one piece of complaining. I don't think Anthony quite knows how beloved that character may end up being."

"He's this character who has been programmed to do something so awful, and it's against his very nature to do so," Anthony says. "Ultimately he's a guy who just wants to be part of the group, he just wants to be part of the band. And, that's way cooler than killing anyone. That's the moral of the story.

"I had such a good time working on it. To be honest, just showing up to set on my first day, I was still in utter disbelief that I was actually part of this series of films that I grew up on. It's hard to say your line when you're looking at Alex and Keanu, and they're like, 'Whoa!', with their arms out. You're you're just thinking to yourself, 'Wow, these guys are amazing!' And then also, what's my line?"

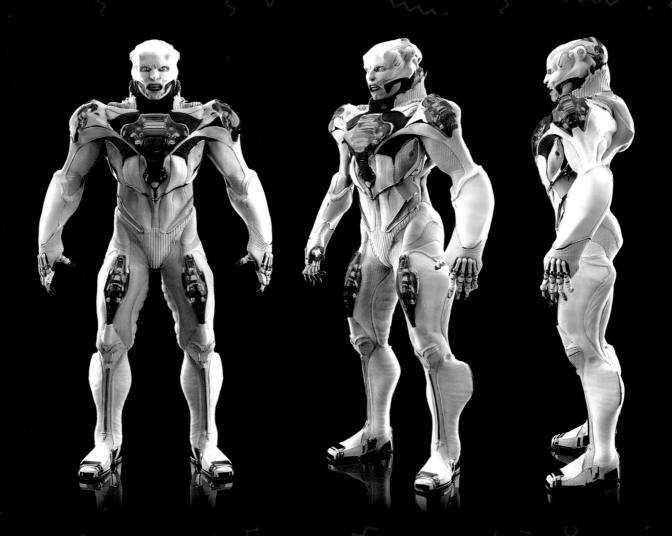

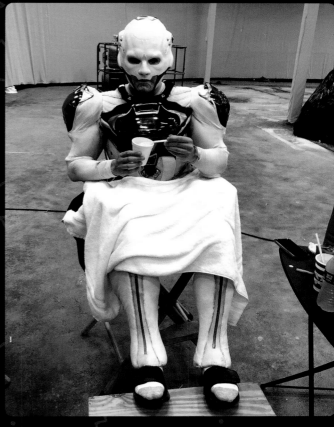

**Above:** Anthony Carrigan cools down on set.

**Left and Below:** Designer Steve Wang and his team create the robot.

**Above and below:** Bill & Ted with the Phone booth, production shots.

**Opposite (top):** Future Bill & Ted, buff and tattooed in the prison yard with some friends.

**Opposite (below):** Bill & Ted peek through the window of Kelly's time travel pod.

# MUSIC

"Music, as a running theme, to me is not inconsistent with the spirit of Bill and Ted," says Ed Solomon. "In that music speaks to people without language. And there is a generosity of spirit to Bill and Ted that seems to transcend the language they speak. Their language is in some ways a very specific Southern California style of language, though in truth, it really isn't. It's something Chris and I essentially made up as we went along. Music reaches people at a different level, and it always felt to me that music to Bill and Ted symbolized freedom. It symbolized reaching other people because they were so desperate. They were so essentially unpopular as teenagers, and yet were so unaware that they were unpopular and uncaring that they were unpopular. Their dream was that their music would be the thing that would bridge them to people. In the third movie, it turns out their music hasn't, and when somebody shows up and says it had better and it had better now, it throws them into a panic. They are forced to assess their lives looking for this song, as if they were in *A Christmas Carol* or *It's a Wonderful Life*. In searching for the song, it's like they're searching for the thing that links people all throughout the world. They're literally looking for a song that will unite the world. The harder they look, of course, the harder it is to find.

"Initially in the first movie, it was just an outgrowth of their natural personalities. They're teenagers. What do they want? They want to be in a rock band that saves the world. But when that gets taken literally and they're told they need to actually do that, suddenly all the lightness

**Above:** The new Wyld Stallyns logo.

goes away, and the pressure is untenable for them. In many ways, the pressure of an adolescent fantasy coming to life doesn't work when you're a middle-aged human being with responsibilities and families and livelihoods."

Music plays an important role in Alex and Keanu's relationship to the characters. "The fun thing about Bill and Ted for us is its relationship to music," Alex says. "The first two films and especially *Face the Music* are anchored around the idea of music and what music can do to liberate and to break down barriers and to create peace and equanimity. The lovely idea here is that it's not a political message. What goes beyond the theme of "Be excellent to each other," is actually a nonverbal idea of

**Above:** The ultimate band plays the song that will save the world.

**Opposite (top left):** Kid Cudi performs, part of the ultimate band.

**Opposite (top right):** Thea and Billie recruit Grom the drummer.

**Opposite (below left):** Death sulks in his music studio in Hell.

**Opposite (below right):** The musicians out of makeup.

music. That music is really one of the great bonds that holds humanity together. It's woven into the plot of this movie very specifically, right down to the characters that our daughters go and try to collect for us; all of them are musicians. It's very different than the previous movies in that way, much more specifically focused around this idea of music, not only from different races, but from different periods of time; how all of those are unified. So music really becomes the metaphor for all of time and space and humanity being one. That's a really fun thing to play with. It's also a very positive thing to play with."

In *Face the Music*, Billie and Thea love music as much as their dads do. Maybe more so. When they decide to help their fathers save the world, music shows them the way.

"Every single one of the actors who played the historical figures was excellent," says Brigette Lundy-Paine. "We started with Jasmine, who plays Jimi Hendrix, and he just nailed it. The first day we shot, Sam and I entering the pod and then going in and seeing Jimi Hendrix playing

on the stage. It was just such incredible experience to see him play, because he had it down. The way he plays and the way he moves, and he captures it so well. It was that experience from then on. Jeremiah playing Louis Armstrong absolutely killed it and watching him with the Preservation Hall Jazz Band was an incredible experience. The same thing with Grom the drummer, with her banging out on those turtle shell drums, and Sharon, who is Linglun – she's actually an old friend of mine from the New York theater scene, so it was just wonderful to work with her. Daniel, who plays Mozart, he brought such a comedy to it. Each of them had their own comedic style, but together we formed a *Wizard of Oz*-like group of wandering misfits. By the end, we spent so much time together on all these crazy sets; we just all knew each other so well. And then, of course, Scott, Kid Cudi. He was a pleasure to work with. Such a wonderful guy, and I really loved getting to know him. That's the thing. Everyone came into this movie so in love with the Bill and Ted world. We all just got to have fun."

"THE GREAT TURNTABLE IS TIPPING."

— KELLY

# PROSTHETIC MAKEUP

"In the second film, Alex, definitely, was really looking forward to playing his own grandmother – playing Bill's grandmother," Keanu recalls. "I enjoy the special effects makeups, but I think Alex enjoys them more. He definitely has more experience with them. I was keen to play all of the different characters and do the makeups. He definitely enjoys it more than me."

"Alex couldn't stop being the old man," says Dean Parisot of *Face the Music*. "He's running around for an hour, coming up to everybody, 'Hey, get away from me!' Keanu's lying in the bed saying, 'Oh, let's hurry.' I said, 'You really hate this, don't you?' He said, 'Yeah, but I'm fine.' Alex loves it, and he's looking at Alex, and Alex is going 'What?' He's giving Alex a hard time. That's the most fun part: those two are great friends and it shows.

"Those prison suits – Alex kept saying, 'I want more pecs' – his suit got bigger and bigger – that thing weighed 40 pounds. There's a moment where he's running around in this giant thing – it's two inches thick. It's like wearing five down coats and it's 100 degrees in Louisiana in the summer. He's roaming all over the place. And he came up to me and I looked in his face and I said, 'Are you okay?' He goes, 'You know, I'm about two seconds away from falling over, could you help me? I gotta stop.' We took him inside, and I thought he was gonna collapse. Keanu

somehow, never said a word. He just has this amazing, super focus and he just blows through it. He also never complained about a thing. It was horrible. We were uncomfortable and I was in a t-shirt."

"I asked Kevin Yagher to make me look like a silver back gorilla." Alex says. "I'd given him photographs of gorillas, and said I want to look like this. So that's what he did. I had this massive suit on, it was 100 degrees and 100 per cent humidity. I was in an altered state, I was so hot and so weighed down by the suit, and so in character, I guess. My brain was really in the mindset of that character – I was just gone. Keanu suggested a line change, and he looked at me and I was streaming sweat. I mean, it was fun, I love doing makeup effects work. And these are the best guys in in the business.

"Bill Corso did my makeup. He's an absolute legend. Bill did my makeup for *Freaked*, which was groundbreaking, and he remained a really good friend. He went on to win the Academy Awards. I was back in the makeup chair doing heavy prosthetics work with Bill and with Kevin Yagher, who did my granny makeup in *Bogus Journey*. Keanu and I went to do the makeup test at Kevin Yagher's shop and he's still got all of the old suits for the Station creatures."

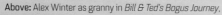

**Above:** Alex Winter as granny in *Bill & Ted's Bogus Journey*.

**Right (above):** Academy Award winning Makeup artist Bill Corso works on Alex Winter as Old Bill.

**Right (below):** Dean Parisot and the crew shoot Keanu Reeves as Old Ted.

**Opposite:** Prison Bill & Ted.

# FANS

"It is without question the reason that *Bill & Ted Face the Music* got made is the fans, period," Ed Solomon emphatically states. "There was skepticism about whether or not the movies would be well-received publicly, and because of social media, because there was a way for people to really gauge fan reaction, it became very clear very quickly that there actually was a market for this. For me specifically, the interaction I had with fans from all over the planet – because on Twitter I had the opportunity to interact with people – it became clear to me how much the movie meant to them. And that was a real shock, really an amazing surprise. And because of that I became dedicated to doing the best I could to give them a movie that would be worthy of the support they've been giving. You know, honestly, they feel like a large extended family. I've said that before, but they truly do."

Solomon continues, "There's a character in the movie referred to as Cyrus Adler, and there's a line Keanu says, 'I went into Cyrus Adler Music,' and that came because a woman posted on Twitter, saying how her father's last words before he died were 'Be excellent to each other. But don't forget to party on!' It knocked me to the floor. I reached out to her and I asked if it was okay that we named him after her father."

Keanu recalls, "Once we all decided to try and tell another story of these characters, it had been seven, eight years, and people would always ask, like, so where is it now? Is it really happening?" He continues, "Alex was really connected to the fanbase and we decided, when it got more real, to send a message to the fans and say thank you for all the interest, because it really did have a positive effect on the studio and the finance, to make it possible. So they were definitely instrumental in that.

"It was [also] really cool to get that response from people working on the film – just how much affection they had for Bill and Ted, whether they'd seen films when they came out or after. It was fun to see some reactions from the crew. Just being like, 'Yeah, I want to be on the show. I want to do this.' To some of the artists, the actor, actresses, 'I can't believe I'm doing Bill and Ted. Excellent!' I haven't had that experience much, so it felt really cool. You want to embrace that feeling; you want to have a good experience. I think we did. It really bonded the crew and the cast together in a really great way really quickly. We're in this together, we're making Bill and Ted."

"When we started to try to get the film financed, a lot of places were not interested." Alex says. "As that road went along, people within that hard core fan base were catching wind of the fact that we had a script. So there was this general sense that this thing was on its way to going somewhere and Keanu started getting asked what was going on in interviews for other projects. He would be quite honest and say that we were trying to get it made, and that just created a groundswell of support from that mostly internet-based fan network of the really die hard fans. They really created an outcry for the film and made it very clear that they wanted another movie, and that went from being a pretty niche group – though we're still probably talking in the hundreds of thousands – to a much larger group, in the millions. Once that happened the financiers and the studios began to realize that this was real and that there was a genuine appetite for the film. That helped us greatly in securing the financing.

"The internet is something I've been involved with since the late eighties. The communities that grew up around the internet that were largely anonymous I found very satisfying, because it didn't matter who I was. It was just about your interests, and no one really knew who you were. It became a very easy and safe way for me to interact with fans. How that manifested itself with Bill and Ted is that some of the community that I found online were Bill and Ted fans. Some of those people – long before we were working on *Face the Music* – started creating Bill and Ted fan sites. One was John Morzen, who created the Bill & Ted 3 web page and eventually the Bill & Ted 3 Facebook page. He was one of the main drivers of our fanbase. Once people caught wind that we were writing the third film, those pages that he created blew up. The Bill & Ted 3 page that Orion now uses is the page that John built. John is a friend who I met over the Internet and he has worked for my company Trouper for years, doing all of the social media work for all of our documentaries.

"I saw Bogus Journey with my brother and sister in the theater when it first came out." John Morzen recalls. "I've wanted to see a third film ever since. I created an online presence for Bill & Ted 3, almost out of wishful thinking. Other fans connected with it, and it showed that we all wanted to see it happen. I'm elated that it actually helped in getting the film made and marketed. For me, to go from growing up watching and loving these films, to becoming a part of the franchise, has been wonderful."

"Because of the sweet nature of the movies, the fans tend to be sweet by nature," Alex says. "They tend to be very good-hearted people, both from the generation that came up with the movies, and a lot of kids whose parents turned them on to the films."

*Bill & Ted Face the Music* made it to the screen on the love and commitment of fans in the industry and in the audience. People like Cyrus Vance, who live by the credo, "Be excellent to each other! And party on, dude!"

**Alma Adler**
@AlmaJA11

Replying to @ed_solomon

My father died in 1992 after a long illness. One of the last things he ever said to me was "be excellent to each other...but party on" thank you ed and chris

1:09 PM · Jan 16, 2019 · Twitter for Android

23 Retweets    562 Likes

---

**Ed Solomon** ✓ @ed_solomon · Jan 16, 2019
Replying to @AlmaJA11
This makes me very emotional. I'm so sorry for the loss of your dad. Thank you (him) for letting us be a small part of your life, through him

♡ 1          ⇄ 2          ♡ 177

---

**Alma Adler** @AlmaJA11 · Jan 16, 2019
Thank you, that means a lot, and makes me happy and sad at the same time.

♡ 1          ⇄          ♡ 100

---

**Ed Solomon** ✓ @ed_solomon · Mar 21, 2019
reading your post again makes me feel the same. what was your dad's name?

♡ 2          ⇄          ♡ 93

---

**Alma Adler** @AlmaJA11 · Mar 21, 2019
Cyrus Adler. He was a great man who spent his life trying to help those in need. Thank you Ed, this means the world to me.

♡ 2          ⇄          ♡ 110

---

**Ed Solomon** ✓ @ed_solomon · Mar 21, 2019
Okay with you if we do this?

> TED
> (beat)
> I went into Taylor Wood Music
> yesterday. I talked to Cyrus.
> He said I could get 64 hundred
> dollars for the Les Paul.
>
> BILL
> What are you saying, Ted?
>
> A pause.
>
> TED

♡ 24          ⇄ 13          ♡ 458

---

**Alma Adler** @AlmaJA11 · Mar 21, 2019
Definitely!!!! I am speechless (which people will tell you is a very rare event)

♡ 1          ⇄          ♡ 173

---

**Ed Solomon** ✓ @ed_solomon · Mar 21, 2019
Sweet. Thanks. :)

♡ 7          ⇄          ♡ 124

---

**Opposite:** Alex Winter and Keanu Reeves in a still from the Hollywood Bowl promotional video for *Face the Music*.

**Above:** Twitter conversation between Ed Solomon and Alma Adler about her father's death.

"...AND PARTY ON, DUDES!"

## AUTHOR'S ACKNOWLEDGEMENTS

The author would like to thank Ed Solomon for years of counsel and friendship, and for recommending me for this bodacious gig; Roland Hall at Welbeck for hiring me and for an excellent experience; Chris Matheson, Dean Parisot, Scott Kroopf and Alex Lebovici for sharing their stories and their support of this project during difficult times; Alex Winter, Keanu Reeves, Kelly Carlin, Anthony Carrigan, Kid Cudi, Stephen Herek, Hal Landon, Jr., Brigette Lundy-Paine, Spyridon Michalakis, William Sadler, Amy Stoch, Samara Weaving for the most excellent interviews; and Bill Corso, Steve Wang, and Kevin Yagher for the interviews and their generous sharing of photos; Dennis Cummings, Cheryl Maisel, Tiffany Malloy, Sophie Canter, Kelli Gallagher, Tim Kressman, Eileen Kwon, and Willa Nelson for their help scheduling interviews and making things happen; Eric Kleifield for supplying marketing materials; and John Morzen for his photography, collaboration and love of all things Bill & Ted.

To keep up to date with Bill & Ted, visit
hiips://www.billandted3.com/
Facebook hiips:/www.facebook.com/BillAndTed3/
Twitter hiips:/twitter.com/BillandTed3
Instagram hiips:/www.instagram.com/billandted3/

## PICTURE CREDITS

Page 9 - Peggy Sirota for *Entertainment Weekly*
Page 10 - Collection of Ed Solomon
Page 12 - Ed Solomon
Page 115 - Peggy Sirota for *Entertainment Weekly*
Page 117 - Bill Corso
Page 120 - Bill Corso
Page 121 - Alex Lebovici
Page 126 (top) - Collection of Ed Solomon
Page 127 - Bill Corso
Page 129 (inset) - John Morzen
Page 146 - Render by Mauricio Ruiz
Page 146 - Steve Wang
Page 147 (upper right) - Alex Lebovici
Page 147 (all others) - Steve Wang
Page 151 (lower right) - Alex Lebovici
Page 156 - Screengrab from Hollywood Bowl video
Page 157 - Screengrab from Twitter
All other *Bill & Ted Face the Music* photographs: Patti Perret/Most Excellent Productions, LLC.